IN Tudor and Stuart times Lady's Bridge was the
It gave access from the town to Assembly Green
on Easter Tuesday the Earl of Shrewsbury, as Lord o
town militia. The Wicker was also the site for the to
the cuckstool, or ducking stool, with two chairs for p
malicious gossip.

Lady's Bridge, built of stone in 1486 to replace an earlier structure, took its name from the Chapel of Our Blessed Lady of the Bridge, a chantry chapel which stood at the bottom of Waingate beneath the castle wall. After the Reformation this chapel fell into disuse and by 1572 was being used as a wool warehouse. In 1589 it was converted into an almshouse for four poor persons, and in 1657 was rebuilt using stone from the demolished castle:

> "for preparing a way to tumble stones for the Almshouse   9d.
> for a rope to draw stones out of the Dungeon   1s. 10d."

Lady's Bridge by W. Botham, 1802

SHEFFIELD Castle, the stronghold of the Lord of the Manor, stood at the confluence of the River Don and the River Sheaf in an area of land bounded on its other sides by a water-filled moat. The moat was crossed by means of a drawbridge which gave access, beneath a gateway flanked by two bastion towers, to the inner bailey. Here stood the main castle building on top of a raised mound, later known as Castle Hill.

Between 1570 and 1584 Sheffield Castle served as one of the prisons for Mary, Queen of Scots, with her retinue of thirty attendants. She was in the custody of George Talbot, 6th Earl of Shrewsbury, on Queen Elizabeth I's instructions.

During the Civil War, Sheffield Castle was garrisoned with Royalist troops, but in the summer of 1644 it surrendered after a siege by Parliamentary forces, ably assisted by Sheffield townspeople. In 1647 Parliament ordered that Sheffield Castle should be *"sleighted and demolished."* So total was the destruction that, today, only a few stones remain as evidence in the cellars of the Castle Markets.

A door from Sheffield Castle, by T. Winder, about 1900 *Sheffield Castle bastion tower plinth, during excavation in 1927*

PART of the Castle complex was the outer bailey containing the Castle Folds, where the sheep were penned, and the Castle Laiths. Here the barns were sited which, along with other storage and service buildings, were set on fire during the Civil War. Fronting Waingate, the ancient wagon road into Sheffield, was Castle Green, said to have been the tournament ground.

Truelove's Gutter, named after an old Sheffield family called Truelove, was a notorious open sewer at the top of Castle Green. It posed a serious threat to householders living there, and in 1694 the Town authorized a payment of £2 to John Webster and William Cuttrell...

"towards their loss by the True love gutter breaking up"

Opposite the Castle Folds lay a broad open space known as the Bullstake, part of the market area, where bulls were baited by dogs, beasts were sold and where the town bull may have stood for hire. From the Bullstake, Dixon Lane led down to the Sheaf Bridge, built in stone in 1596 and giving access to Sheffield Park.

Castle Green by W. Botham, 1802

BEYOND Sheaf Bridge lay the Castle Orchards. Here in 1666 the Shrewsbury Hospital was built for the reception of twenty-four poor persons of the town of Sheffield, 50 years after the death of its founder, Gilbert, 7th Earl of Shrewsbury. It enjoyed open views into Sheffield Park which in 1637 extended over 2,460 acres and where 1,000 fallow deer and 200 *"deer of antler"* were chased for sport and meat by the Lord of the Manor's private hunting party. However, Gilbert, 7th Earl of Shrewsbury...

> *"was wont on every yeare, on a certayne day, to have many bucks lodged in a meadow neare the towne side, about a mile in compasse, to which place repaired almost all the apron-men [cutlers] of the parish and had liberty to kill and carry away as many as they could with their hands, and did kill some tymes 20, and had money given them for wine by the Earle."*

So began the tradition of the annual Cutlers' Feast.

Sheffield Park was also famed for its huge oak trees. John Evelyn writing in 1646 remarked:

> *"in the same park a tree was cut which when laid aside flat upon level ground 2 men on horseback could not see over it one another's hat crowns."*

Broad avenues of oak and walnut trees led through the Park to Sheffield Manor.

Sheffield Manor by R. Hopkinson, 1818

S HEFFIELD Manor, as described in 1620, stood...

"on a hill in the midst of the park, being fairly built with stone and timber, with an inward court and an outward court, 2 gardens and 3 yeards, containing 4 acres, 1 rood, 15 perches."

What is now a ruined manor house began as a medieval hunting lodge which in the 16th century was enlarged to a more splendid residence and an alternative to Sheffield Castle, the principal seat of the Earls of Shrewsbury.

In 1529 Cardinal Wolsey, in disgrace with Henry VIII, stayed at the Manor as a guest of George Talbot, 4th Earl of Shrewsbury. Wolsey's gentleman-usher, George Cavendish, observed how the Earl...

"conducted my Lorde to a faire gallerey, where was in the further ende thereof a goodlie tower with lodgings where my Lorde was lodged. There was also in the mideste of the said gallery a travers of sarcenett [curtain] drawne so yt the one ende thereof was preserved for my Lorde and the other for the Earle. And once everie daye my Lorde of Shrewsbury would repair unto him and commune with him, sitting upon a bench in a great windowe in the gallerey."

Whilst this sharing of principal apartments was, perhaps, adequate for an occasional visitor, the formality of Elizabethan hospitality required that persons of rank should have separate state rooms and separate lodgings for themselves and their household.

<u>Ruins of Sheffield Manor</u> by A Wilson, 1898

The Turret House, Manor Lodge by E. Goodwin, 1795

Turret House Banqueting Room, about 1890

ACCORDINGLY, when Mary, Queen of Scots, was placed in the custody of George, 6th Earl of Shrewsbury, he was obliged to enlarge the Manor to accommodate her and her household. In 1582 there are references to *"the quenes gallery there"* and *"the Quenes kitchen at ye lodge"* as distinct from the Earl's own accommodation.

The Turret House, standing in the outer courtyard, is the only roofed building which survives at Sheffield Manor and contains many original features including fine plasterwork. Built in 1574, it appears to have formed part of a grandiose rebuilding scheme which recent archaeological excavation by Sheffield City Museums has uncovered. This included an imposing new front entrance to the house flanked by brick-faced octagonal towers and a new garden layout.

19th century romantics supposed that the Turret House was built as a prison for Mary, Queen of Scots. In fact, it is too small and does not correspond to the written accounts of the considerable suite of rooms which she and her household occupied. Nor is it appropriate as a place of safe custody for a dangerous political prisoner, as it is sited on the garden boundary wall next to the main gate. The Turret House probably served as a gatehouse to Sheffield Manor and also as a hunting tower, a fashion in deer parks in the 16th century. On the top floor is a delightful room where the Earl's guests could take shelter after having viewed the chase across Sheffield Park from the Turret House roof and partake of a banquet, which in the 16th century consisted of a small meal of sweet desserts and wine.

Seen from such a high vantage point, Sheffield town appeared as a mass of huddled buildings clustering around the Parish Church of St. Peter with its steeple, topped by a weathercock, towering over all. Around the town lay open fields, woodland and moors as far as the eye could see.

In the town narrow streets were lined with houses and shops and, behind them, reached by even narrower passages, were makeshift cottages, cutlery workshops, stables, cowhouses, malthouses, bakehouses and swine hulls. Beyond these lay orchards, gardens and crofts. Today, names such as Orchard Street, Mulberry Street and Fig Tree Lane are the only reminders.

ACH householder was responsible for disposing of his own rubbish and sewage. Failure to do so resulted in fines. In 1578 a group of householders had...

"leyd certeyne maynor or dounge in the hye stretes contrary to a payne layd wherefore everye of them is amerced 4d."

In 1609, blacksmiths and cutlers were similarly guilty. It was ordered that...

"all those householders dwelling in the church lane shall remove, take and carry all such myre, smythie sleck and filth, being in the towne streete against their houses, and not to cast any sweepings of ther houses, smythies sleck or other things which shall hinder the water passage."

Street cleaning was a constant problem which the appointment of a town scavenger in 1687 went some way towards solving. He was employed by the twelve Capital Burgesses, a body constituted in 1554 to regulate the public affairs of the town.

North Perspective View of the Town of Sheffield, by T. Oughtibridge, 1737

THE Town Hall where they met stood at the corner of the churchyard, at the top of High Street, adjacent to houses known as Prior Row. Although it was extensively repaired in 1659, it was too small to act as a common meeting place for the town's business assemblies. Until 1700, when a new Town Hall was built on the same site, large meetings were held in the Parish Church.

In 1590 George Talbot, the 6th Earl, was buried in the Shrewsbury Chapel vault in the Parish Church. Arthur Mower of Woodseats recorded in his diary how the funeral was more sumptuously performed than...

"was ever to any afore in these countrys: and the assembly to see the same was marvellous both of nobility, gentry and country folks, and poor folks without number."

Above 20,000 persons were present, of whom some 8,000 poor received dole, as was customary. The funeral was held at night, in January, and fires were lit for warmth and light. The Burgery Records note that three onlookers...

"were slayne with the fall of ii trees that were burned downe at my lordes funerall the 13th January 1590."

In 1700, at the chancel door, William Walker, the supposed executioner of King Charles I, was interred. He had long lived at Darnall, *"a mysterious stranger."*

The 6th Earl's tomb in the Shrewsbury Chapel

THE Hall in the Ponds, now known as the Old Queen's Head inn after Mary, Queen of Scots, was probably built by the 4th Earl of Shrewsbury in the late years of the 15th century. It was an appendage to the Castle, as the 1582 inventory of the contents of the Castle also lists the furnishings *"in the hawle at the Poandes"*:

*"Item peces of paynted hangings, wyndowe peces, and chymney peces, of canves, xx
Item a long borde standing on trestles
Item buffett formes, ii, buffet stoules, i, cupboardes, i
Item a stylle, a flaggen
Item iii olde pewter dysshes and ii spytts"*

19th century tradition maintained that the Hall was the laundry to the Castle. It was clearly not that but rather a sumptuously decorated dining room.

The Ponds was the name given to the large, flat, marshy area alongside the River Sheaf, where artificial ponds, no doubt stocked with fish to serve the Castle, also provided the water to power the Lord of the Manor's corn-mill. Given that shooting wildfowl with crossbows was a noble sport, it seems likely that the Hall was built as a lodge for taking refreshment after fowling and fishing in the Ponds.

Old Hall in the Ponds by B. K. Dale, 1815

THE Hall in the Ponds was originally more extensive than it is now, and early plans show it to have been L-shaped. Architecturally, it is a high-quality timber-framed building with much costly carved detail. In particular, a number of corbels carved as heads are noteworthy, as is the carved Gothic quatrefoil ornament on the underside of what was the main window lintel. It has a projecting upper storey which, in turn, once contained jettied windows.

Timber-framed buildings such as this were constructed by carpenters using freshly cut oak trees, as the wood was easier to work while still green. The crooked appearance of most timber-framed buildings is due to the timber drying out after the building had been erected. Sometimes an owner would insist, in the building contract, that the carpenters came back to refix the window frames once the drying out was complete.

The main structural timbers were generally shaped on site. As each timber was finished to the required size, its joints were numbered in relation to the other timbers against which it would be fitted. Once all the timbers making up the frame of the house had been made, the numbered joints were then readily put together and secured by wooden pegs. This assembling of all the parts, known as the house-rearing, could usually be accomplished in a day. It was an occasion for much festivity. Successive stages involved the infilling of the frame with lath and plaster and the roofing with stone slabs.

Hall in the Ponds, about 1900

Snig Hill by A. Wilson, 1895

SHEFFIELD in the 16th century consisted almost entirely of timber-framed buildings, as stone was too costly for any but the most important structures. With their narrow, overhanging frontages, timber-framed houses stood at the roadside soaring upwards and stretching backwards in their long burgage plots.

The type is well illustrated by the houses which used to stand on Snig Hill, just below the site of the Irish Cross. This was first mentioned in 1499 and marked the part of the market in which foreigners could sell their goods. It also acted as a boundary marker for the district in which they lived. Scotland Feast, held at the traditional time of the May Games, survived in this area until 1826.

Snig Hill takes its name from the practice of putting a *"snig"* or length of wood through the back wheels of carts going downhill, to act as a brake. The hill was the main route, leading to the Town Corn-mill at Millsands, for heavy wagons laden with grain. It was also the way out of town along West Bar where stood the Workhouse, built by the Town about 1630 for the care of twenty poor children. They had to earn their keep, and in 1633 money was given...

"To one who came from Chappell [en-le-Frith] to have taught children to knitt."

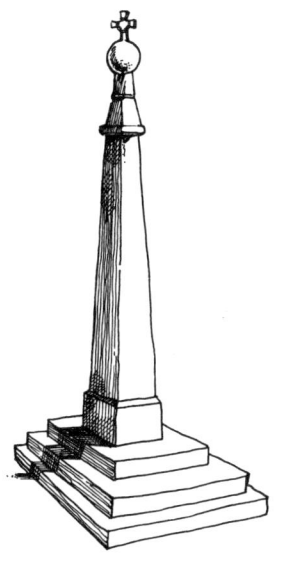

The Irish Cross

Snig Hill, by F. Mottershaw, 1886

13

TIMBER-FRAMED houses in narrow streets meant that the risk of fire was a constant threat and, as late as 1676, the Town Burgesses agreed that the Lord of the Manor...

"shall be moved to consent to the removall of the Common Bakehouse, and the building of another in a more convenient place, where it may be less dangerous to the town."

Their fears were not without foundation, for in 1697 payment was authorized...

"To Nathaniel Meares for kitts [buckets] when the bakehouse was on fyer."

The bakehouse probably stood in Pudding Lane, the passage which ran from the Bullstake to Market Place along the back of the Shambles. In the Market Place was the Market Cross where, in 1650 after the Civil War, baptisms and marriages were publicly performed. It was flanked on one side by the Pillory, erected in 1572, and on the other by the stocks which were later transferred to the Church gates.

In the High Street, just down from the Market Cross, was a fine half-timbered house at the corner of Change Alley. This may have been the building erected in 1574 by William Dickenson, Bailiff to the Earl of Shrewsbury, as in 1706 one of the rooms in this corner block was still known as the Bailiff's Chamber.

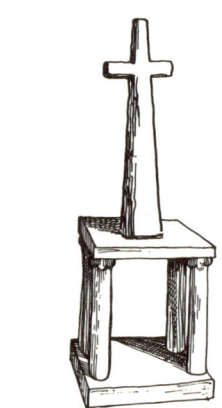

Market Cross

Old House at the corner of High Street and Change Alley, by F. Mottershaw, 1886

14

Broomhall by E. Blore, 1820

Pitsmoor Hall by W. Botham, 1802

IN the 16th century, as in town so in the surrounding countryside, timber-framing was the traditional method of construction for farmhouses and barns. Pitsmoor Hall was particularly fine, with carved barge-boards to its gables topped by fancy wooden finials. Broomhall, which still survives, was the home of the Jessop family, whilst Bishops' House at Norton Lees, now one of Sheffield City Museums, is the outstanding example which can still be seen today.

Built around 1500, Bishops' House consists of an east wing containing the Hall, the centre of household life, which was originally open to the roof and a kitchen and kitchen chamber. About 1550 a cross-wing was added to provide the family with private apartments, chief of which was the parlour.

The original owners and builders are not known but, as the house is not large enough to have been an important manor house, it is likely to have been built as a home for a member of the minor gentry or a prosperous yeoman farmer. Documents and pictures record that barns and outbuildings were once attached.

Old Hall at Norton Lees [Bishops' House], by E. Blore, 1823

THE Bishops traditionally thought to have lived here were two brothers, John Blythe, Bishop of Salisbury (1494–1499) and Geoffrey Blythe, Bishop of Lichfield and Coventry (1503–1533). There is no proof for this story and the name Bishops' House is itself of recent origin.

However, a minor branch of the Blythe family did live here in the early 17th century and William Blythe, whose initials and the date 1627 appear in the panelling, was a farmer and perhaps the largest local producer of scythes before the Civil War. He was well able to afford the improvements he made to the house, which included the installation of fireplaces, wainscot panelling and decorative plasterwork. He died in 1631, a wealthy and prosperous yeoman for his time.

His son, another William Blythe, inherited the property. He was a Captain in the Parliamentary Army, and one of the two local officers put in charge of the demolition of Sheffield Castle in 1648. Captain Blythe paid £3 for *"bords and plaster"* from the Castle and may have used these materials in the addition which he made to Bishops' House.

Since suitable oak for building was by this time scarce, the new extension, providing two additional rooms with fireplaces, a cellar and an improved staircase, was built in stone. In fact, by the 1650s stone had become the common building material in Sheffield. Some stone-built houses had made their appearance as early as 1630 when it was said that they had been dug out of their cellars, the stone so excavated being used for the walls.

Bishops' House, by Theophilus Smith, about 1870

STONE-BUILT cottages on the Little Hill at the top of Campo Lane bore the datestone 1630. They were built in a busy part of Sheffield near the Pinfold, an enclosed piece of ground to which stray animals, particularly pigs found rooting amongst street refuse, were shepherded by the Pinder. Careless owners had to pay a fine to redeem their impounded animals. However, judging from the numerous references to mending the Pinfold, it must have been common practice to break down the door and steal back the impounded animal without paying the fine.

At the junction of Pinfold Lane with Church Lane stood the Townhead Cross and the Townhead Well. In 1609, to prevent pollution of the drinking water, it was ordered that...

"no person or persons shall at anytime hereafter wash any clothes, calfe heads, calfe meates or swyne meates, or other things within 3 yarde of the Townhead well."

Wellgate, which led down to Broad Lane, intersected Campo Lane at a point where the Grammar School had been established in the mid-16th century. Below street level, with steps leading down to the doorway, it was a dismal place. In 1648, the same year that the Castle was demolished, it too was taken down and rebuilt with materials from the Castle.

Little Hill at the top of Campo Lane by W. Botham, 1802

BLIND Lane, running alongside Brelsforth Orchards, connected Townhead with Balm Green, a large open space at the top of Fargate. Balm Green, found as *"Le Balne"* in early documents, is thought to take its name from the Latin *balneum*, meaning a place for bathing. Traditionally it was also the place where the herb, balm, grew and which was *"most singular to heale up greene woundes that are cut with iron."* In a town of metal workers balm was a necessary medicinal plant.

In Balm Green stood Barker's Pool, a large square reservoir for the storage of water supplied by springs. A barker was one who prepared oak tree bark in water for tanning leather and, whilst a Barker of Balm is mentioned in 1434, the earliest reference to the pool is not until 1567. Townspeople depended on the pool for a source of fresh water to supplement supplies from pumps and public wells and for putting out fires in the town.

In 1572 the pool was enclosed by a stone wall and fitted with a shuttle or sluice gate. On occasions this was opened to flush the channels in the middle of the streets of all the filth and refuse that had accumulated. The Bellman gave notice of the exact time the cleansing waters would be released and people made ready with buckets and brooms to wash house frontages and rake garbage into the drains to be carried away on the flood. A torrent of water lasting half an hour would pass down Fargate and High Street to the Market Place where it dispersed by way of Truelove's Gutter and Water Lane to the low-lying area known as Under-the-Water.

Townhead Cross

Cottages on Balm Green by W. Botham, 1802

Balm Green cottages, 1900

U NDER-THE-WATER was prone to flooding not only when the River Don was high but whenever the sink at the end of Lady's Bridge became blocked with the refuse swilled out of town. On these occasions surface water drainage was a danger and in 1683 the Burgery Records mention payments...

"For cleaning the Almshouse after a great flood."

The road from Balm Green to Little Sheffield Moor was known as Coal Pit Lane and here, in the late 17th century, a small house was erected with a door lintel bearing the initials LJS and the crossed daggers of the Cutlers' Company. It was once popularly assumed that this house had been the old Cutlers' Hall. In fact, it was one of several houses in Sheffield displaying the Cutlers' Arms which their owners had erected with pride during their terms of office as Master Cutler. One lintel, with the Cutlers' Arms and WRL 1694, is now in the City Museums' collections, whilst another, dated 1692 from West Bar, was removed to the Cutlers' Hall in 1912.

Cutler's House in Coal Pit Lane by W. Topham, 1877

THE cutlery trade in Sheffield throughout the 16th century was controlled by regulations issued by the Court of the Lord of the Manor. By the early 17th century the cutlers' desire for greater control of their own affairs led to the formation of the Cutlers' Company by Act of Incorporation in 1624, with a Master Cutler, two Wardens, six Searchers and twenty-four Assistants.

The Cutlers' Company rented the upper chamber of a prestigious stone-built town house in Fargate, later known as the Cutlers' Inn, in which to hold its meetings. This served the Company well until 1638 when, having purchased a plot of land in Church Lane, it set about erecting its own hall. The money for building was raised by subscriptions and by selling company stock. Amongst the local families who contributed to the building fund were the Brights of Carbrook and the Spencers of Attercliffe. These wealthy subscribers took pride in their own houses and patronized a skilled group of woodcarvers and plasterers whose work can still be seen in the interiors of a number of local buildings.

Cutlers' Inn, Fargate, Artist unknown, about 1810

Carbrook Hall by E. Blore, 1819

Carbrook Hall Parlour, about 1910

THE stone-built wing of Carbrook Hall, which still survives, contains two remarkable early 17th century rooms. The Parlour, once the principal apartment of the house, is lined with geometric oak panelling, divided by pilasters and surmounted by a carved frieze.

ABOVE this is a moulded plaster frieze and a superb decorative plaster ceiling. The carved oak fireplace overmantel is almost identical to one from Norton House, dated 1623, and now in the Cutlers' Hall.

The parlour chamber contains stencilled wainscot panelling, remnants of decorative plasterwork and a grand renaissance overmantel. There is good reason to believe that Carbrook Hall was decorated by craftsmen who had worked at Bolsover Castle.

Stephen Bright, who added this wing to Carbrook Hall in about 1620, was Bailiff of Hallamshire and became Lord of the Manor of Ecclesall in 1638. He died in 1642 and was succeeded at Carbrook by his son, John Bright, probably the most active person for the Parliamentary cause during the Civil War in Sheffield. He was a Colonel in the army under Sir Thomas Fairfax and was appointed Governor of Sheffield Castle after its surrender. In 1650 he retired from military life and returned to the management of his large estates.

The Bright family were staunch Puritans. Stephen Bright of Carbrook, together with his brother John, the Vicar of Sheffield, played a prominent part in the erection of the Chapel which still stands at Hill Top on Attercliffe Common. It was built in 1629, at the cost of the inhabitants of Attercliffe, and consecrated in 1636. In 1649 it served a community of 250 families who had previously had to travel to the Parish Church in Sheffield for services.

Attercliffe Chapel by H. Thompson, about 1840

THE Spencer family of Attercliffe, near neighbours of the Brights, shared the same religious and political views. William Spencer, Lord of the Manor of Darnall from 1641, provided funds towards the building and endowment of Attercliffe Chapel, whilst his son, William, was a Lieutenant-Colonel in the Parliamentary army. Their home, Attercliffe Hall, suffered bombardment by Royalist troops during the Civil War when the house was plundered and Colonel Spencer imprisoned. Sadly now demolished, Attercliffe Hall had claim to be one of the more important buildings in the parish of Sheffield.

It was an extensive house, later refaced in brick, which contained a large chamber decorated with elaborate plasterwork in the local style of the 1620s and 1630s. Over the fireplace was a plaque with the Puritan text:

*"What soever thou dost take
in hande thinke of the ende
and seldom so shalt thou offend."*

This was a highly appropriate verse for the purpose to which this chamber was put in the later 17th century, after the Spencers vacated the Hall.

Attercliffe Hall, about 1910

Attercliffe Hall chamber, about 1910

Attercliffe Hall chamber, about 1910

IN 1686 Richard Frankland took a lease of Attercliffe Hall and established a training Academy, principally to educate students for the Nonconformist ministry. It is likely that the plastered chamber was the Academy room where the teaching took place. After three years, Frankland was succeeded by the Rev. Timothy Jollie, who was later Minister of the Upper Chapel, Sheffield, and who renamed the Academy Christ's College. Many famous people were educated here, including Secker, later Archbishop of Canterbury, Sanderson, the blind Oxford Professor of Mathematics, and Halley, the astronomer of Halley's Comet fame.

The major part of Attercliffe Hall was taken down in 1868, but the wing containing the Academy room survived, split into a row of cottages, until the final demolition in 1934. The same fate, unfortunately, befell another remarkable house, Greenhill Hall, as recently as 1964.

From the outside, Greenhill Hall presented a picturesque appearance with its gables, mullioned windows protected by hood moulds, and its front doorway distinguished by a four-centred reeded arch.

Greenhill Hall by W. Topham, 1880

THERE is no record of when Greenhill Hall was built, but it was probably erected by James Bullock, described in documents as of Greenhill and Beauchief, in the early 17th century. The Bullocks were a wealthy family with interests in water-mills and scythe smithies on the River Sheaf, and were keen to consolidate their property holdings in the area. By 1624 they had acquired all the lands which comprised the Manor of Norton and it seems likely that Greenhill Hall, if not rebuilt at this time, was refurbished in the latest style.

The Oak Room at Greenhill Hall was a sumptuous Jacobean Parlour displaying a confident handling of renaissance ornament. The Bullock coat of arms was proudly set in the elaborate woodcarving of the fireplace surround and the family crest in the decorative plasterwork of the ceiling. A high level of craftsmanship, such as could be seen here, was not, however, confined to grand houses alone. Quite ordinary cottages, such as those on Oakes Green at Attercliffe, were built with considerable care and attention to architectural detail.

The Oak Room, Greenhill Hall, 1964

Old House, Attercliffe by W. Botham, 1800

Old Cottages, Oakes Green, Attercliffe Common, 1905

ONE small house worthy of particular attention was the Old House near Washford Bridge on the Attercliffe Road. Later known as the Fleur-de-lis inn and now demolished, it was one of the most interesting small houses erected during the later 17th century in Sheffield.

Originally consisting of a living room and a parlour with two bedrooms above, it was built of locally-quarried rubble stone laid in flat courses with architectural details, such as quoins at the wall corners, cut from gritstone. Gritstone was also used in the rebuilding of the adjoining Washford Bridge in 1670.

Washford Bridge Old House doorway, about 1920

Washford Bridge Old House by W. Topham, 1877

THE door lintel was carved with an inverted heart-shaped shield, within which was the date 1671 and the initials ER. These stood for Elizabeth Roades, a widow. In an Estate Rental of 1671 appears the entry:

"For stone got out of Dick Bank for Widow Roades house at Attercliffe, 3s. 0d."

Elizabeth Barnsley had married Richard Roades in 1624. He was tenant of three cutlers' wheels, called Roades or Royds Mill which, when he died in 1638, became her means of livelihood for raising her family of seven children.

At the age of 66, after a lifetime of hard work and many years of widowhood, Elizabeth Roades gave up the business she had run for thirty-three years and built her retirement home where she died eight years later in 1679. Recalling the fashions of her youth, the parlour featured a plasterwork overmantel with her initials and the date 1676. By that time, however, such features were becoming out of date. Even stone itself, by then the common building material, was facing a new challenge from brick.

Plasterwork overmantel, Washford Bridge Old House, about 1920

AT SHEFFIELD Manor brick had been used for prestige building in Elizabethan times, but it had never been used for ordinary dwellings in the town because first timber, and then stone, had been readily available. When, about 1696, the first brick house in Sheffield was built in Pepper Alley, just off Fargate, there was consternation amongst the townpeople. It is reported that thousands of persons went to see it, and that...

"it was viewed by the inhabitants with wonder and ridicule, they supposing it to be built of such perishable materials that it must soon yield to destruction."

Of course it did not fall down, but it was pulled down in 1837. At the time it was, indeed, a talking point; something new and different. It was an indication of things to come, but also a sign that Sheffield would never be the same again.

Brick house in Pepper Alley by W. Botham, 1802